Amy & Toph,

Great to see you both.

You're wedding was as much
fun to shoot as the ones I've helped
Liz with. Best wishes,
Michelle Phillips

Weddings

by Tara Guérard

Weddings

by Tara Guérard

tara p. guérard

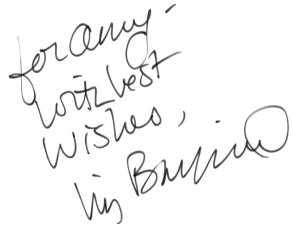

for Amy –
with best
wishes,
Liz Banfield

Tara Guérard

photography by Liz Banfield

GIBBS SMITH
TO ENRICH AND INSPIRE HUMANKIND
Salt Lake City | Charleston | Santa Fe | Santa Barbara

First Edition
14 13 12 11 10   5 4 3 2

Text © 2010 Tara Guérard
Photographs © 2010 Liz Banfield

Published by
Gibbs Smith
P.O. Box 667
Layton, Utah 84041

1.800.835.4993 orders
www.gibbs-smith.com

Designed by Julia O'Neal Shuman
Printed and bound in China

Gibbs Smith books are printed on either recycled, 100% post-consumer waste, FSC-certified
papers or on paper produced from a 100% certified sustainable forest/controlled wood
source.

Library of Congress Cataloging-in-Publication Data

Guérard, Tara.
  Weddings by Tara Guérard / Tara Guérard ; photographs by Liz Banfield. — 1st ed.
    p. cm.
  ISBN-13: 978-1-4236-0737-3
  ISBN-10: 1-4236-0737-6
  1. Weddings—Planning. 2. Wedding decorations. I. Title.
  HQ745.G84 2010
  395.2'2—dc22

                    2009029746

Cover: *Roger Vivier shoes worn by Olivia Mansfield on her wedding day.* Page 2: *A bridal bouquet of gardenias, roses, lisianthus, and phalaenopsis orchids.* Right: *An intimate historic garden wedding reception with pink peonies, pale pink linens with black piping, and chandeliers with black shades.* Facing: *Kristen and Josh share their first dance as Mr. and Mrs. LeQuire.* Pages 8–9: *The view from cocktail hour, the perfect sunset on the marsh of Kiawah Island.*

Contents

We at Soirée by Tara Guérard love weddings! We love the entire process—from design and planning to the execution of the big event. For us, the divine is in the details! On the heels of our successful first book, *Southern Weddings,* the following pages provide examples of extraordinary real weddings that we were fortunate to oversee. It is our hope that readers enjoy and find inspiration—as we did—from each of the featured couples and their once-in-a-lifetime celebrations.

This book is dedicated to the beautiful brides and dashing grooms who brought our vision to life. Thank you! Thank you also to Elizabeth Cash, Kate Little, and Anne Pope for their assistance in writing this book, and to Julia Shuman for her graphic design. Also, many thanks to our fabulous, talented, dependable vendors—you always make us look good. And, finally, a huge thank-you to my devoted Soirée team, who for over a decade have been the backbone of the company. We would not be where we are today without you!

Tara Guérard

Above, Left: *An excited Olivia and Zach just after the ceremony.* Above, Right: *Boxwoods-and-flowers cake by Sylvia Weinstock.* Facing, Left: *Father of the bride peeping out the front door just before walking his daughter down the aisle.* Facing, Right: *A poem loved by the bride and used for wedding wishes.*

Under the Oaks

Olivia Mansfield and Zach Wall

Mr.andMrs.

College sweethearts at Washington & Lee University, Olivia and Zach had a storybook courtship that led them to post-grad life in New York City. Zach set the stage for his surprise marriage proposal with a New Year's visit to the Mansfields' beloved vacation home in Sea Island, Georgia. Undeterred by a dreary day at the beach, he popped the question and set off the family's holiday festivities with an early champagne toast and dinner to ring in the new couple—and the new year.

The ceremony was held under centuries-old oaks, which created a lush backdrop. Right: The bride's bouquet was filled with parrot tulips and, of course, the groom had a boutonniere to match.

Below, Left: *Lanterns topped with fresh flowers were hung from tree limbs by boxwood garland, creating a glamorous and unexpected altar piece.* Below, Right: *A view of the all-white dance floor and lounge.* Facing, Left: *To help construct an aisle, we used wrought-iron hooks, boxwood garlands, and fresh flower nosegays.* Facing, Right: *A view of the poolside cocktail area.*

The Scene   Design and Décor

Olivia envisioned a sophisticated traditional wedding held on the grounds of her family's home—our favorite kind of celebration site! We loved the colors she chose for the décor: pinks, oranges, pastels, and champagne. We designed an interlocking "M" and "W" logo, mixed her colors, and placed boxwoods everywhere. From the ceremony in the front garden to cocktails in the house and around the pool, to dinner and dancing under the tent, Olivia and Zach's at-home wedding was magical.

Bright Idea

Floating Monogram

We've often seen floating floral shapes and candles before, but we wanted a fresh idea to bring the pool into the décor. We custom made the "M" and "W" monogram out of styrofoam and covered it in hearty pink and orange carnations to bring in that pop of color. It was the perfect unexpected detail!

Tapas Stations

....

Tenderloin of Beef and Venison
with piped mashed potatoes and confetti asparagus

Bacon-Wrapped Quail
stuffed with pepper cheese over butternut squash gratin

Wild Boar Tenderloin
served over cornbread dressing

Mini Chicken Pot Pies

Homemade Mac and Cheese

Beef Short Ribs
over rich creamy cheese grits, and whole fried okra

Black-Eyed Peas
with tomato pudding, collards, and lacy cake

Above: *Servers rolled cheese carts throughout the reception tent.*
Right: *Mother of the Bride in orange Oscar de la Renta, takes a break, eats, and chats with a friend over the music of the band.*
Facing: *Bar specialty drinks calligraphied on acrylic signs and 21 Club Burgers.*

21ClubBurger

Adapted from New York's famous 21 Club, this was one of our passed hors d'oeuvres and one of Olivia's favorites.

2½ lbs freshly ground beef
Olive oil
Salt and pepper
1 tb dried thyme
4 slices rustic Italian bread, cut into ½-inch-thick slices
2 ripe beefsteak tomatoes, cut into ½-inch-thick slices
1 red onion, cut into ½-inch-thick slices

Shape the meat into 4 round patties about 1½ inches thick. Lightly brush both sides with oil and sprinkle with salt and pepper. Cook on the grill over medium heat, for about 7 to 8 minutes per side. Brush the bread, tomato, and onion slices with olive oil and sprinkle with thyme. Season the onion and tomato with salt and pepper. Place the bread, onion, and tomato on the grill and lightly grill both sides.

To serve, place each burger on a slice of grilled bread and top with slices of tomato and onion. *Serves 4*

"*We kept it green* by making our own birdseed recipe so that the same kinds of flowers and grasses *would continue to grow* within this family's lawn after it was tossed at the bride and groom."

Making time to take a couple of photos before the ceremony is a way to have timeless black-and-white photography from your wedding day.

LOVEBIRDS
goodbye!

SoiréeSignatures

Wedding Cake Conservatory

We love making the wedding cake the centerpiece of the party. In a tent covering this much ground, making sure the cake became a focal point was a challenge. So within the tent, we constructed a wrought-iron conservatory, draped it with boxwood garlands to match the handmade cake details, and set out tivoli lights. We then custom made an acrylic table that we could arrange large pots underneath. The cake appeared as if it were floating on boxwoods—gorgeous!

Monogrammed Napkins

Our monogram logo design on napkins was an easy detail. Champagne in hues that match the wedding colors is a nice detail as well. Why not?

Guest Book

Avoid long lines at large weddings and give your guests a chance to write wishes while waiting for the ceremony to start. We filled little mesh bags with a pen, a card to write wishes on, rose petals to throw at the end of the ceremony, and a miniature wedding program. We love to be efficient!

Favors

The wedding favors flew off the shelves, literally. The women at this wedding loved having a wrap for a late night stroll by the pool, and flip-flops were an excuse to shed uncomfortable heels.

Birdcage

The birdcage dangled from a tree limb by the front door so that guests could drop their wishes inside. We simply gathered notes at the end of the evening and made a traditional guest book for the bride and groom.

Happily Ever After

Olivia and Zach were a dream to work with. After only three months to plan their at-home wedding (and Olivia being an only daughter!), it all came together with exceptional food, fun, and beautiful weather. Even the family pup, Max, had a blast at the party! While many elements from this wedding played on the things that Olivia and Zach loved about living in New York City, they have now decided to return to the South to be closer to their families.

Facing: *Sofas and ottomans are great places for guests to rest while attending cocktail/buffet-style wedding receptions.* Above: *Bride and groom changed clothes and headed off into the night after a perfect evening.* Right: *Mr. Mansfield whirls his daughter around the dance floor.*

Above, Left: *Hillary and her flower girl make faces right before the wedding.* Right: *A chandelier from the reception symbolizes the glamour.* Facing, Left: *Casa Blanca lilies cut short and tightly packed in a vase made the dance lounge smell heavenly.* Right: *Bride and groom during their first dance.*

Glamour Girl

Hillary Rich and Will Herring

Mr.andMrs.

Hillary and Will were classic college sweethearts, dating throughout school and for several years following. The couple became engaged during what was to be an early Christmas celebration before departing for their respective hometowns for the holiday. Will took his bride-to-be completely by surprise with a ring he had designed especially for the momentous occasion. They were later married at historic Drayton Hall plantation, surrounded under the oaks by friends and family.

Hillary and her dog, Tallulah, just after the ceremony. Both were excited to add Will to their family! Right: Will kissing his bride. A guest holding our uniquely shaped ceremony program.

TheScene   Design and Décor

Lavender and light blue. Wow! This color combination was cool, refreshing, tantalizing, and glamorous. We designed three spaces for guests to flow through: a lavender-toned clear cocktail tent with fabric swags and chandeliers; a blue- and silver-hued dinner tent with a custom ceiling gobo that mimicked the pattern from the printed materials; and an ultra-glam all-white dancing lounge with a luxurious fabric liner, chic sofa's, and a gleaming dance floor. Hillary and Will's wedding was not to be missed.

BrightIdea

Shoe Bags

For your amenity bags, try giving something your guests can keep and reuse—not only in the contents, but in the packaging itself. We found canvas travel shoe bags in Hillary's wedding colors which we filled with goodies and personalized by adding letterpress tags. Guests could repack these and easily take them home.

TastingMenu

....

Paillard of Local Grouper
with a cracked black pepper crust
served with a spinach soufflé and mushroom duxelles
finished with a fresh thyme sprig

Sautéed Local Jumbo White Shrimp
over a saffron-scented ragoût of johns island tomatoes,
scallions, and sweet onions
served over a stone-ground yellow grits cake

Salad of Mixed Baby Greens with Duck Confit
tiny green lentils, and split creek farms goat cheese
tossed with a mustard vinaigrette

Herb-Dijon-Crusted Rack of Colorado Lamb
with a minted zinfandel reduction
over roasted yukon gold potatoes

Above: *Parents of the bride enjoying dinner.*
Right: *The wedding cake in hues of blue and lavender with designs from the bride's dress. The cake stand was custom made for the wedding.* Facing, Left: *Banana Split Cheesecake served in glass votives for after dinner.* Right: *Clear acrylic menu cards etched by The Lettered Olive.*

BananaSplitCheesecake

1½ lbs soft cream cheese ½ tsp vanilla extract ½ cup light brown sugar
2 cups granulated sugar 1 tb banana extract ½ tsp lemon juice
1 tsp minced lemon zest ½ tsp salt 2 cups Oreo wafer crumbs
½ cup all purpose flour 6 eggs 4 cups fresh whipped cream
2 tbs cornstarch 2 bananas 48 fresh mint leaves

Place cream cheese, sugar, and lemon zest in mixer bowl with paddle. Beat on low until soft; scrape down sides. Add flour, cornstarch, vanilla and banana extracts, and salt. Beat on medium for 2 minutes; scrape down sides. Add eggs. Beat 2 to 3 minutes. Pour batter into prepared springform pan. Place in preheated 225-degree F oven on a sheet pan for 1 hour. Reduce heat to 200 degrees F and cook for 1 hour. Check internal temperature; it should be 175 degrees F. Remove and let cool for 1 hour, then refrigerate for 12 hours overnight. To caramelize bananas, peel and slice into ½-inch slices. Toss in brown sugar. Sprinkle with lemon juice and toss until sugar is dissolved.

To Assemble: Sprinkle crumbs into the bottom of the glasses. Place chilled cake into mixer and beat until smooth and creamy. Place in pastry bag with star tip and pipe onto crumbs. Add 1 or 2 slices of caramelized banana. Pipe with fresh whipped cream. Top each with 2 mint leaves. *Makes 24 individual votives*

We made our favors *eco-friendly* by using local flowers and by giving away all of the table centerpieces. We had enough *for each couple* to take one home.

Our all-white after-dinner lounge. Right: Favors were engraved mint julep cups filled with lilacs and sweet peas that had been table centerpieces.

SoiréeSignatures

Purse Flower

Corsages may remain the traditional preference of your grandmother, but mothers and other members of the wedding party might be looking for something a little more modern. Purse flowers, like this one using a Cattleya orchid, are always a hit. Another twist on this—a wrist flower. Tie the flowers with a beautiful matching ribbon and the piece becomes a bold fashion statement.

Going Away

We are always trying to think of something new to send off our brides and grooms. Here we re-covered silly string cans with labels that read "We got silly at Hillary and Will's wedding," and they did!

Aisle Flowers

While a rustic scene can often be pretty, for our "glamour girl" we needed to gussy up this plantation lawn. We loved the simplicity of these monochromatic single-bloom orchid garlands, and they created a dramatic aisle that didn't seem out of place for the outdoor ceremony.

Save the Date

Not only were these lavender and blue letterpress booklets gorgeous, they were also clever. Most people like to put "save the date" cards somewhere they can see them as a reminder, so these had a perforated card that guests could remove and put anywhere.

Paper Flowers

Even though they're some of the last things you and your guests will see that night, your exit details can provide some of the most memorable photos. Making these large paper flowers is easy to do yourself, they are affordable, and they make a lasting impression.

HappilyEverAfter

Despite a rain shower that delayed the ceremony by half an hour and threatened our beautiful décor, Hillary and Will's wedding ceremony and reception went on to be one of the most breathtaking events we've done yet. We finished off the weekend by working with Hillary's parents on a "day after" brunch at their house, where everyone gushed over all the details and relived stories. Because Hillary and Will are a local Charleston couple, we are still able to catch up with our bride; she often stops by to check in and remind us how much she enjoyed planning her wedding.

Facing: *Still happy, even after the silly string!* Above: *The bride's shoes. Before the wedding, each bridesmaid signed the bottom.* Right: *Bride and groom stroll, heading towards cocktail hour.*

Short Story

The Wedding Celebration of Kristen Skatell and Josh Lequiré

Inspiration for Kristen's wedding came from a magazine photo she brought to us. From this photo we were able to gather an idea of what the bride had in mind for her special day. We designed a classic-but-modern wedding incorporating her chosen colors of blue, black, and white. Details included black handblown Italian glass chandeliers, letterpress invitations and a wedding cake to mimic its design, carnations in memory of Kristen's mother, and blueberries in champagne. Kristen and Josh's evening began with cocktails in the garden, followed by dinner in a historic mansion and dancing under an enchanted tent.

Above, Left: *A glimpse of the after-dinner lounge with the sun setting over the marsh in the background.*
Right: *Hand calligraphed table number signs tied with a ribbon and dressed up with Kermit mums.*
Facing, Left: *Custom-designed white and green table linens edged in pink satin.* Right: *Megan and Scott sharing an intimate moment together after the ceremony.*

SeptemberSplendor

Megan Embrescia and Scott Peckham

Mr. and Mrs.

Busy professionals living in Los Angeles, Megan and Scott turned to the matchmaking service of their generation—the Internet—to find companionship and hopefully love. Taking a chance on one another's attractive profile pictures and some listed shared interests, the two arranged to meet for cocktails at a hotel in Beverly Hills. They clicked and extended the blind date to dinner. Theirs was truly a match! A fun-filled six months later, Scott proposed outside the couple's newly purchased home in Hollywood Hills, the lights of L.A. twinkling below.

Left: *In place of one wedding cake for dessert after dinner, the bride and groom opted to have several cakes with different flavors.* Right: *To produce a fun club room, the pavilion was lined in fabric, carpeted, and lit in green hues.* Facing: *Crystal chandeliers hung from the pink-lined tent.*

TheScene   Design and Décor

The bride wanted a preppy-chic pink and green affair. Therefore we transformed a rustic riverside park on Kiawah Island into "splendor on the marsh." The guests flowed from the oyster tabby where the ceremony was held, to the boardwalk for cocktails, to a beautiful pink-lined dinner tent. The evening ended at the pavilion with dancing in the green lounge.

Bright Idea

Butler Boxes

Rather than using the standard escort table, we designed clever butler boxes. Each guest received a box that contained a custom letterpress menu card, an adorable table assignment card, and a card to paste their Polaroid picture (taken earlier) with a place to write the bride and groom a "well wish." We then wrapped each box in matching paper and a pink satin ribbon. A hand calligraphed name tag for each guest was affixed by the ribbon.

On the Menu

....

Seared Atlantic Tuna
truffled gold potato, soft poached egg,
pickle of baby beans and lemon chive aioli

Roasted Butternut Squash Ravioli
sweet pea purée and baby arugula
porcini mushrooms, herbed brown butter

Preserved Tomato Salad
humboldt fog cheese and grilled sourdough bread
slightly dressed greens, cracked olive compote

Petite Filet of Beef and Local Carolina Grouper
asparagus butter, creamed morels, and roasted corn
roasted baby carrots and carolina gold rice

Above: *Green chandeliers hung in the after-dinner lounge.* Right: *Bride at her Kiawah home, about to leave for the ceremony.* Facing: *A tasting of hors d'oeuvres for the bride and groom to eat while taking pictures. The Lettered Olive designed the butler box, displaying the menu card and table assignments.*

FreshFigs *with Cracked Pepper Goat Cheese*

⅓ cup sherry vinegar or cider vinegar

1 tb molasses

2 tsps extra virgin olive oil

¼ tsp salt

¼ cup (1 ounce) crumbled goat cheese

4 large (dark-skinned) fresh figs, halved

¼ tsp freshly ground black pepper

Combine first four ingredients in a medium bowl, stirring with a whisk. Gently stir in the goat cheese and place a half teaspoon on each fig. Sprinkle with freshly ground pepper. This recipe can be served cold, or wrapped in prosciutto and finished in an oven at 425 degrees F for 5 minutes. *Serves 4*

Keep it green by using *recyclable materials*. Recycled paper bags held marshmallows to make s'mores on the bonfire.

The ring bearer, Luke Flynn, entertains himself during the ceremony. Facing: marshmallows for roasting marshside, sticker by The Lettered Olive.

Soirée Signatures

Designer Fabrics

To bring originality and character to your wedding, find a pattern in your favorite colors that can be incorporated throughout. For example, use the patterned fabric on your chair covers, table linens, and throw pillows. The green and white material we used here helped pull all the details together.

Customize Personal Flowers

Leftover fabric was fashioned into bouquet wraps and a ring bearer pillow. Little surprise details like these make memorable photographs.

Guest Box

We like to repackage everything to match. It is important to think of all the details! As a substitute to a guest bag, we had boxes made in our custom patterned paper. Each box included edible treats, an informative local book, custom water bottles, the guest booklet containing all the wedding and island activities, and his-and-her bathing suit–shaped cookies in pink and green.

Flower Girl

We are always trying to come up with inventive flower pieces for our flower girls. To be different, we hot-glued Kermit mums and pink Nerines on a headband for each flower girl.

Bottled Lemonade

So many brides want to pass out drinks to their guests before the ceremony. To make this a special element (and to not have the problem of glasses tipping over and spilling), we designed and packaged a glass bottle. Each was filled with our delicious Soirée signature drink, low-country lemonade.

Happily Ever After

We could not have ordered a more picturesque wedding day. The sunset was miraculous, and wild butterflies even showed up during the ceremony. Warm water breezes kept dinner mystic, and late-night vibes kept guests dancing until the very end of this splendid reception. The father of the bride said it was the best wedding he had ever attended.

Facing: *Bride and groom chair covers by Soirée.* Above: *A happy father of the bride.* Right: *As the bride and groom departed, guests waved flags. The American flag for the bride and the Canadian flag to pay tribute to the groom's heritage. Bon voyage!*

Above, Left: *Double-sided square wreaths made from lush peonies and garden roses.* Right: *Beautiful bridesmaids hold hand-tied bouquets.* Facing, Left: *The bride and groom's monogrammed cake, custom designed by Jim Smeal.* Right: *The bride, Ann E., on her way to the wedding ceremony.*

Wedding Rice

Ann E. Rice and Tucker Ervin

Mr.andMrs.

Ann E. Rice and Tucker Ervin are a special match. High school sweethearts who dated throughout their teenage years and early twenties, the pair never veered from their vision of life together. On their annual Colorado holiday vacation with Ann E.'s parents and a few close friends, Tucker proposed at the steps of the Telluride courthouse. This was the location of many of the couple's past New Year's Eve celebrations and despite the frigid temperatures, a perfect setting for their engagement. Ann E. followed in the footsteps of her well-known father, Joe, and graduated from the University of South Carolina's School of Law in the weeks just before walking down the aisle. It was amazing to see our bride prepare simultaneously for both the biggest day of her life and her future career!

Facing: The flower-wall entrance was a new twist on the traditional wedding reception portrait. Right: Ann E. and Tucker arrive by horse-drawn carriage to the front-lawn reception.

The Scene   Design and Décor

The task at hand was to build and decorate a tented affair (over 23,000 square feet) in less than a week for 1,200 guests. Our décor elements included silver, blue, and white fabrics used for curtains, upholstered furniture, carpets, linens, and, of course, flowers. Custom-built cocktail bars and food stations were flawlessly executed with details such as silk bottoms, hanging sputnik lights, sumptuous food, and creatively mixed drinks. The back lawn was transformed into a sleek, modern setting, which afterwards was the talk of the town.

BrightIdea

Embroidered Bouquet Ribbon

Not only did we individually box and wrap wedding party flowers, we also personalized each bouquet ribbon by embroidering the attendant's monogram on each. This is a clever and inexpensive gesture to remind your closest friends and family how much they are appreciated.

Cocktail Buffet

....

Sautéed Local Shrimp
*in a tasso ham gravy with fresh silver queen corn
and organic yellow grits cake*

Beef Tenderloin Medallions
with spinach and lump cake ragoût and béarnaise sauce

Southern Fried Chicken Medallions
over buttered mashed potatoes with green tomato chow-chow

Pickled Shrimp with Artichokes and Olives

Chilled Open-Faced Lobster Rolls

Pork and Veggie Stir-Fry

Homemade Mac and Cheese

Sesame Seared Tuna

Above: *To-die-for Homemade Mac and Cheese in ramekins with cocktail forks.* Right: *Over fifty servers lined the entrance to cocktail hour, patiently waiting to serve guests with their choice of champagne or cucumber water and hors d'oeuvres.* Facing, Left: *Sesame Seared Tuna.* Right: *Pork and Veggie Stir Fry served in Chinese take-out containers with chopsticks.*

Sesame Seared Tuna

¼ cup white sesame seeds
¼ cup black sesame seeds
Salt and pepper to taste
1 tb sesame oil
2 (8-oz) tuna loins, cut in half

Place a large nonstick pan over high heat until hot. Combine sesame seeds in a bowl; season with salt and pepper. Drizzle oil in pan. Lightly salt tuna; dredge in sesame mixture. Reduce heat to medium and place tuna in pan. Sear until lightly browned, about 2 minutes. Flip; cook 2 minutes more. Remove from heat and let rest for a few minutes before serving. *Serves 4*

One large wedding cake was placed in the center of the table and surrounded with nine additional smaller cakes on acrylic tables with monogrammed runners. Right: Father of the bride and Ann E. arrive through the front doors of the church.

To stay green, after the night was over, *all of the fabrics, carpets, and other hard goods were donated* to Habitat for Humanity, ensuring they would have a second life.

Soirée Signatures

Printing

The Lettered Olive, Soirée's sister company, designed an elegant letterpress invitation using charcoal-colored ink. It is a Soirée signature to create one-of-a-kind printing accoutrements for each of our weddings—from save-the-dates to ceremony programs. We keep the details consistent from start to finish.

Well Wishes

Guests left messages on monogrammed paper swatches and slipped them into "rice" bowls at six different locations. At the end of the night, we gathered the cards and attached them to paper, which in turn were made into custom guest books for the bride and groom. It was a fabulous solution for a wedding attended by 1,200 guests!

Restroom Tent

Who would ever think a picture of restroom trailers under a tent would be a wedding book topic! We were so proud that all five of our large restroom trailers (including one handicap facility) could be set up in the middle of a plantation field and still look so lovely.

Rice to Throw

Because our bride's maiden name was "Rice," we couldn't resist the traditional act of throwing rice at the end of the wedding reception. However, rice is very harmful to birds, which is why it is prohibited by many venues. So, to be creative and give the illusion of rice, we used orzo pasta in its place.

Flower Garden Wall

A wall of flowers is a great way to disguise the inevitable tricky spots that arise in ceremony layouts. Here, we wanted to hide the organist's head and have a gorgeous backdrop for the bride and groom's ceremony photos, as well as have something different in the church. We constructed this flower wall out of plywood and covered every square inch with peonies and roses.

HappilyEverAfter

Ann E. and Tucker were a great match for Soirée. They each had their own specific vision for what they wanted their weekend to reflect. Their traditional Southern background but modern style was a perfect fit for our own creative sensibility. The groom's black, white, and fuschia Friday-night celebration mimicked a super-swish nightclub, and the wedding was full of ultra-sleek lighting and clean lines—from the bars to the custom furniture and linens. One of the retro-modern chandeliers used at the reception now hangs in the couple's new New York City apartment—a great testament to our efforts.

Facing: *Ann E. and Tucker depart their magical evening all smiles.* Above: *Mother and father of the bride share laughter and tears as the bride and groom dance.* Right: *A view of the dinner tent.*

Night Before

The Rehearsal Dinner of Hillary Rich and Will Herring

Rehearsal dinners and Friday-night parties are well worth an honorable mention. The wedding eve often produces some of the most unforgettable events of the weekend. This evening included an intimate dinner for family and friends, followed by a late-night dance/lounge for all out-of-town guests. We used a bright color scheme to tie the two parties together with details including escort/butler cards displayed in yellow millet-filled painted trays, Gerbera daisies in colored glass vases for the late-night décor, amazing sweets for guests to enjoy while dancing, and colorful letterpress invitations and menus.

Above, Left: *Engraved invitations in gold lettering with hand-painted edges and a logo-embossed bellyband.* Right: *A view of cocktail hour on the veranda overlooking the harbor.* Facing, Left: *The centerpieces for the head table were made from peonies and roses. Gold taper candles created soft lighting, and etched glassware was our gift to the bride.* Right: *Lawton and Eric at the altar.*

Bands of Gold

Lawton Ginn and Eric Yon

Mr. and Mrs.

While they attended the same school for years, Lawton and Eric did not meet until a common high school class brought them together. Friends at the start of the semester, they passed study hall notes and later shared their first kiss at the spring prom. The couple ventured to the College of Charleston, where their romance continued for another four years. Shortly after graduation, Eric led Lawton down a rose petal–strewn path, where he popped the question—and champagne—in her mother's picturesque courtyard garden.

Below: *The head table during dinner.* Facing:
*The bar, with white wooden top and eggplant
satin fabric bottom built by Soirée.*

TheScene   Design and Décor

Redecorating an unattractive space for an event is one of our favorite projects. This old ballroom, with its linoleum floors and drop-tiled ceiling, resembled a cafeteria. To transform the space into an elegant wedding reception of gold and eggplant, we covered the walls and ceiling with fabric and carpeted the floor. Not only did it become a breathtaking venue but it softened the acoustics to keep the affair romantic and intimate.

BrightIdea

Two in One

We combined the favors and place cards into one unit. Each guest received a little candy box filled with delicious macaroons, with the flavors matching the wedding colors—pecan with bourbon vanilla buttercream and violet with cassis buttercream. A kind message was included that read "the sweetest pair." Each box was wrapped in printed paper and had a name tag attached. The favors were placed on the guests' table settings to also serve as their place card.

DinnerMenu

....

Sweet Corn and Crayfish Chowder

Pan-Seared Grouper
*with a lemon herb sauce over a bacon and smoked gouda
grit cake and vegetable ragoût*

Tuscan Rubbed Beef Tenderloin
*with mashed potatoes, creamed spinach,
and a smoked tomato bordelaise*

Above: *Macaroon favor/place card boxes
packaged by Soirée and The Lettered Olive.* Right:
*Tables set for a queen. Table numbers were old
Charleston street names.* Facing, Left: *Mother of
the bride and mother of the groom clap after listen-
ing to the loving toasts.* Right: *The specialty drink
was named using the bride's nickname, "Lawdy."*

Lawdy Toddie

Our bride, Lawton, claims she can't live without this widely popular sweet tea vodka!

Per Glass:
Ice cubes
2 ounces of Sweet Tea Vodka (preferably Firefly)
Still water
Lemon wedge

Mix all ingredients in the glass. Squeeze juice from the lemon wedge on top. Must be served ice cold, just like nonalcoholic sweet tea. We like to keep the vodka in the freezer so it's always chilled.

Help save the Earth while decorating your wedding by using *eco-friendly paints.*

The dining room just before guests entered. Right: The church front entrance with painted leaves and rose-filled kissing balls.

SoiréeSignatures

Guest Amenities

We all relish the simple pleasures in life and take advantage of small luxuries. That being said, when it comes to designing events, it's important to think of the guests first. We like to make sure they have a drink in their hand, have a comfortable place to sit, and even have a wrap available if it becomes a bit chilly.

Sparklers

Engraved matchboxes are a great favor idea. Not only are they practical for your guests but they become fun reminders of your wedding when used again later. Note that sparklers can be dangerous, so it is important to purchase the smallest size and the variety that doesn't smoke.

Bride's Bouquet

Hand-tied bouquets are always dreamy. Lawton made hers especially significant and beautiful by incorporating her godmother's cameo, which was pinned to her ribbon. It also served as her "something borrowed."

Chair Flowers

A perfect, simple peony can go a long way. Spruce up a nondescript chair with a flower and satin ribbon. Be sure to cut the ribbon ends to finish the look. We like to cut an inside "v" on one side and an outside "v" on the other.

Social Room

One of the best ways to get your reception into high gear is to get your guests out of their seats—literally. Move dancing to another section after dinner. We have found that wedding guests can become antsy at a dinner table all night, so we like to design a social room for mingling.

Happily Ever After

Lawton had been planning her wedding to Eric since they were teenagers. This made it very clear to me how special we wanted their night to be. Also, Lawton and Eric are famous amongst friends and families for their parties, so we had to make this the ultimate culmination of events! After living in Charleston their entire lives, both Lawton and Eric received job opportunities that took them to Williamsburg, Virginia. Their goal is to end up back in Charleston to start a family together, so we look forward to celebrating on their return.

Facing: *Lawton and Eric wave good-bye to friends and family.* Above: *Guests send the bride and groom off with sparklers.* Left: *A sweet moment between father and daughter on the way to the ceremony.*

Above, Left: *A bridesmaid bouquet, hand tied with garden roses, tulips, and orchids.* Right: *Megan and Clayton walking on the beach from their house to the reception.* Facing, Left: *Simple buttercream cake with bands of edible sand dollars.* Right: *A view of the dinner tent from the beach amongst Palmetto trees.*

SeaIslandSoirée

Megan McGraw and Clayton Mozingo

Mr.andMrs.

A twist of fate and a rescheduled finance class brought Megan and Clayton together in an empty classroom at the College of Charleston. Clayton proposed six years later on a pristine Bermuda beach, significant to the couple, as Megan's family had visited there since the early 1900s. The pair married on Sea Island, Georgia, another special coastal spot—the site of Megan's grandparents' 1949 honeymoon and her parents' summer home.

The Scene   Design and Décor

The decor elements envisioned by our clients included the colors of the sand, seashells, and the ocean. They wanted the setting to be simple yet sophisticated. We created an island-inspired scene with natural fibers such as seagrass, rattan, and the like. Even the ceiling tent was made from bamboo! Our seaside fantasy dinner and reception passed with flying colors.

BrightIdea

Upper-Level Flooring

Our clients wanted dinner on the beach, so we gave them the next best thing: a tent on the front lawn of Sea Island's Ocean Forest Club. We raised the floor three to four feet in the air so that the guests had a panoramic view over the sand dunes to the ocean. It was a breathtaking sight!

CocktailHour

....

Tuna Tartare on Wontons

Grandpa's Cheese Puffs *(by the McGraw family)*

Lobster Salad in Profiterole

Smoked Salmon on Toast Points

Traditional Shrimp Cocktail

Crab Maison

Oyster Shooters

Fried Shrimp and Fried Oysters
Chef frying to order

Above: *An almost-devoured slice of wedding cake.* Right: *An oceanside dinner tablesetting, dressed with seashells, flowers, and candles.* Facing, Left: *Crab Maison in scallop shells on ice.* Right: *Shot glasses filled with oysters and gazpacho on ice.*

Crab Maison

⅓ cup mayonnaise
3 tbs French dressing
3 scallions, chopped fine
1 tsp small capers, drained
½ tsp chopped parsley
1 lb lump crabmeat
6 lettuce cups
12 slices tomato
Lemon juice

For French Dressing:
½ cup white wine vinegar
2 tbs creole mustard or other
1½ cups olive oil
½ tsp salt
1½ tsps ground white pepper

To make French Dressing, mix together vinegar and mustard. Slowly whisk in olive oil, a little at a time, to form an emulsion. Season with salt and pepper.

To assemble salad, mix together mayonnaise, dressing, scallions, capers, and parsley. Fold in crabmeat carefully to preserve the lumps. Divide into six equal portions and serve each in a lettuce cup with two slices of tomato on the side. Squeeze lemon juice over the salad just before serving. *Serves 6*

To stay eco-friendly, we borrowed *sand and shells from the beach* to arrange our table centerpieces and returned them to the beach afterward.

Bamboo ceilings and sea grass flooring kept our seaside reception green and natural.

SoiréeSignatures

It's All in the Details

To create a consistent look for this wedding, we repeated the same seashell accessory throughout the décor elements. For example, rather than using typical striped plastic drink stirrers, we found clear acrylic swizzle sticks and glued a miniature seashell to each. Voilà, seashell chic! It's easy to go overboard with this concept, so keep the details small in scale.

Seashell Signage

We must drive our caterers crazy with passed hors d'oeuvres signage! However, it is courteous to inform your guests of what is being served. For the display, we poured small seashells into clear votives and wedged a wooden dowel with a sign glued to the top in each.

Shadowbox Bar

Sand and seashells were arranged in the shadowbox bars to continue our theme. These also made a great conversation piece for guests while drinks were being made.

Table Names

We love to have fun with table numbers and names at every wedding. For this dinner, each table was named for a seashell. Even the printed signage was fashioned in the shell's appropriate shape, color, and design.

Beach Butler Cards

To keep the seating cards protected from the beach breezes, we set them up inside the club where guests could pick them up during cocktail hour. We filled shallow clear glass vases with beach sand, hot glued assorted seashells to the tent cards, and even adorned the table with starfish and matching ribbon.

HappilyEverAfter

Both mother and bride are interior designers and have a keen eye for how things should look. For the reception, they each wanted something different, and it was exciting for us to be able to use key elements from our surroundings and also think outside the box to create a different tent interior. It was also fun for the family, who have a home near the reception venue, to watch the progress under the tent leading up to the big night. The bamboo ceiling was one of the biggest challenges yet for the Soirée team, but the gasps from everyone when they saw it was that little reminder that tells us it was worth it!

Facing: *Well wishes, or "footprints in the sand," are always a treat to read after the honeymoon.* Above: *The cheerful bride and groom departing their reception.* Right: *One of the most delightful surprises for your guests is to supply them with take-home boxes for leftover wedding cake.*

Night Before

The Rehearsal Dinner of Carter Samis and Fred Fellers

If you are lucky enough to have your rehearsal dinner party fall on Halloween night, have fun with it! The décor elements here included fog machines, tombstones, white miniature butler card pumpkins, hat by Leigh Magar, vampire teeth, scary servers, trick-or-treat to-go containers, candy bars, spooky decorations, eerie music, true-to-life skeletons dressed as bride and groom, and silver jack-o'-lanterns.

Above, Left: *Children's boxes.* Right: *Dark chocolate wedding cake enhanced with ostrich feathers.*
Facing, Left: *Feather table numbers.* Right: *Bride's bluebird and Vendela roses bouquet, wrapped with ostrich feathers.*

WarmandFuzzy

LaTashia Jones and Melvin Drayton

Mr.andMrs.

Though LaTashia and Melvin's first date led to a serious romance, the couple took some time in introducing their respective children into the relationship—six months to be exact. The first outing with the blended Jones and Drayton families was a success; LaTashia and Melvin knew their love would last when everyone instantly connected. After several years of dating, Melvin asked LaTashia's daughter, Raven, to help him choose a ring for her mother. He proposed to LaTashia on Christmas Eve and she happily accepted, but the date was left open-ended. Months later, LaTashia spied her dream wedding gown—a sign that the timing was right—and let the prospective groom know she was ready to walk down the aisle.

TheScene   Design and Décor

The bride chose lavender, in memory of her late daughter. In addition, the champagne hue, fuzzy feathers, and a Greek key pattern created a playful and unique look for the event. A traditional family-style buffet, dancing to favorite tunes, and an engaging children's table resulted in a night to remember.

BrightIdea

Remembering Loved Ones

A great and intimate way of honoring someone special is to embroider their initials on the bride's bouquet ribbon. It is important to memorialize loved ones who can't be with you on your special day.

SupperBuffet

....

Mrs. Bessie's Meatballs

Southern-Style Chicken Drumettes

Charcuterie Assortment

Picnic Pasta

Charleston Red Rice

Pole Beans Almondine

Gourmet Cheeses and Local Fresh Fruits

Homemade Buttermilk Biscuits

Southern Sweet Tea

Above: *Some of the young guests sipping miniature hot chocolates at the children's table.* Right: *Place settings included feather napkin rings and custom chocolate bar favors.* Facing, Left: *Custom picks were made to match the wedding design.* Right: *Sweet Tea with sugar rims was passed to guests upon arrival.*

Southern Sweet Tea

2 cups cold water
3 family-size regular tea bags (Luzianne Tea preferred)
1 lump sugar and a little more for the rim of each glass

Place the two cups water in a pot and add the tea bags. Bring to a boil and remove from heat. Pour warm tea into empty pitcher. Add the sugar and stir until dissolved. Fill remaining pitcher with cold water.

To serve, slightly moisten the rim of each glass and twist in sugar. Fill with ice cubes and pour in freshly brewed tea. *Makes 1 pitcher*

Keep it green by *refurbishing old* accessories and not purchasing new items. We covered cast-off glass cylinders with *printed recycled paper* to give our table décor a fresh look.

Facing: *Boutonnieres for the groomsmen.*
Above: *Hot chocolate desserts served in espresso cups with chocolate stick stirrers and whipped cream.*

SoiréeSignatures

Sweet Treats

We love designing custom logos for our brides and grooms. It can be as simple as LaTashia and Melvin's L and M. Again, using their Greek key element and their monograms, we repackaged candy bars that served as guest favors. It is an inexpensive and delicious surprise for your guests.

Ring Bearer Pillow

We designed the ring bearer pillow to match the décor by wrapping the top of a box with the printed paper and sewing a small pillow in the Greek key pattern.

Flower Girl Basket

We used the remaining bottom of the box from the ring bearer pillow to make the flower girl basket. We covered the box in paper, then simply added holes for the ribbon handles and filled the box with rose petals.

Petal Headband

From ordinary to extraordinary—a plain store-bought plastic headband became a little girl's fashion statement! We took individual rose petals and created the perfect shaped and size rose to complement a young person's head.

Children's Box

To keep your young guests occupied and entertained, give them matching boxes filled with games or puzzles, coloring books, crayons, and candy treats. We even made little tags printed with the children's names so they felt that it was a special gift just for them!

HappilyEverAfter

The wedding of LaTashia and Melvin was a long time in the making. The two united their families through this special day in which their children played a huge part. At last, LaTashia and Melvin united not only their relationship but a family as well. We revel in the fact that we were able to help make their dream wedding a reality for family and friends to enjoy. Here's to once-in-a-lifetime memories and celebrations!

Facing: *The bride and groom have an intimate moment while standing on the piazza of the United States Custom House.* Above: *The perfect mother of the bride wrist flower.* Right: *A lounge seat perspective of the dining room.*

Above, Left: *A portrait of the bride.* Right: *The candlelit path to the reception tent.* Facing, Left: *Tulips and gardenias bundled for the bridesmaids' bouquet.* Right: *A Jim Smeal cake masterpiece.*

Eyelet Evening

Elizabeth VanWagenen and Barton Dyson

Mr.andMrs.

Young, carefree, and single, Elizabeth and Barton met among their social circle on Daniel Island, South Carolina, and became good friends over a period of time. Elizabeth was always struck by what a gentleman Barton was and knew he would one day be a "catch" for some lucky girl. One lazy afternoon, she spontaneously asked Barton to join her for a movie, an event that became the couple's "aha" moment. Something clicked after the theater, and the pair emerged with a new perspective on their relationship. After four years of dating, Elizabeth and Barton celebrated their marriage, and shared their celebration with many of the same friends whom they had known from the early days of their romance.

Facing: *Elizabeth and Barton merrily walking to their reception.* Left: *A processional of bridesmaids.* Right: *Flower girl headband with blue ribbon and a gardenia.*

The Scene   Design and Décor

The décor inspiration was Elizabeth's eyelet wedding dress. Therefore, we had everything eyelet, including the save the dates, invitations, plates, linens, curtains, and lamps.

BrightIdea

Eyelet Umbrellas

We really do not like wasting anything! Eyelet umbrellas were made from leftover fabric from the linens and runners. A little labor intensive, yes, but well worth the effort.

Hors d'Oeuvres

....

Tuna Tartare on a Wonton Crisp

Fried Quail on Cornbread

Tomato Bisque Drizzled with Basil Oil
in espresso cups

Mini Grilled Pimento Cheese Sandwiches

Crisp Oyster on Toast Point
with remoulade sauce

Deviled Egg Half with Black Caviar

JBC Picked Shrimp

Above: *Eyelet lamps floated above the bar.*
Right: *The dinner was held riverside and under
a clear-top tent. There were eyelet runners
and eyelet bands on linens.* Facing, Left: *The
first course was a sampling of chilled seafood.*
Right: *A sign guiding guests to the reception
tent after the ceremony.*

JBCPickledShrimp

1 cup apple cider vinegar	½ tb minced garlic
1 cup olive oil	¼ cup freshly chopped parsley
2 tbs sugar	½ cup freshly chopped scallion
1½ tbs horseradish	1 cup pitted kalamata olives
1½ tbs Dijon mustard	1 cup halved artichoke hearts *(save juice)*
1 tb kosher salt	½ cup juice from artichokes
1 tb lemon zest	½ cup thinly sliced red onion
1 tb cracked black pepper	2 lbs cooked, peeled shrimp
1 tb oregano	

Whisk together all ingredients except shrimp. Pour over shrimp and stir. Cover and refrigerate at least 4 to 6 hours or overnight. *Makes 8 appetizer servings*

Save money and stay environmentally conscious by forgoing a generator and *using candlelight* whenever possible.

Facing: *Elizabeth with the flower girls and junior bridesmaids.* Right: *Seating was available for guests taking a stroll by the river.*

SoiréeSignatures

In Lieu of Favors

The bride and groom made a contribution toward medical expenses of Elizabeth's young cousin (pictured above), who suffers

from a genetic disorder. Information about her and a picture were secured within the place card envelope at each guest's seat.

Eyelet-Wrapped Invitations

A delicate, ornate letterpress invitation suite wrapped in eyelet paper and ribbons was designed just for Elizabeth. We even used the same design on her wedding cake.

Altar Idea

Traditional flower altarpieces are not required. Just enhance an existing structure with a bit of creativity. We strung ribbons, orchids, and lanterns over an old oak tree limb to create this altar. During the ceremony, the breeze picked up and the ribbons swayed romantically as the backdrop.

Wishes That Stick

Guest books can be ordinary. Be creative! We made blank covered magnets and included directions for writing "wishes that stick" to the bride and groom for guests to attach to the magnetic board used for escort/butler cards.

Magnet Butler Cards

The same board was decorated with eyelet ribbons that held magnet escort cards in alphabetical order. A pretty detail that entertained guests during cocktail hour.

Happily Ever After

Our first meeting with Elizabeth developed a gorgeous, simple, modern, and romantic wedding plan. She envisioned a ceremony with a classical violinist, spring breezes, and a glorious sunset. For the reception Elizabeth visualized candles galore, chandeliers, and lovely lounges. It was our pleasure to make all her dreams come true. The entire day and evening were flawlessly breathtaking.

Facing: *The Dysons delighted at dinner.*
Above: *Elizabeth's bouquet.* Right: *The couple's first dance as Mr. and Mrs.*

ShortStory

The Wedding Celebration of Mary Martin Walker and Richard Roth

Your wedding doesn't have to be about color. Mary Martin and Richard were ultra-traditional and wanted a black-tie affair with all white flowers and a touch of a natural green hue to incorporate into the décor. They liked the idea of bringing in some modern updates, so with the lounge and some bold black-and-white-patterned pillows, we were able to keep the low-key color scheme current. We also used a "Mr. and Mrs." graphic from some printed cocktail napkins as inspiration. We incorporated the phrase into cookies, cocktail napkins, cute cards, the "just married" sign, and so on.

Above, Left: *A twist on the typical black-and-white dance floor.* Right: *Red rose kissing balls hung from the trees along the aisle.* Facing, Left: *Andrea and Nick making their way to dinner after the Badeken, which signifies the unveiling of the bride.* Right: *Letterpress invitations with handwritten calligraphy.*

RosesareRed

Andrea Zucker and Nicolas Muzin

Mr.andMrs.

Love blossomed quickly between Andrea and Nick while the young professionals were pursuing their respective careers in Washington, D.C. Soon after they began dating, Nick visited the Zuckers' home in Charleston, South Carolina, for the Thanksgiving holiday and asked for Andrea's hand in marriage. With her father's blessing, Nick arranged a surprise trip to Israel, where he proposed to Andrea at the Western Wall in Jerusalem—a sacred spot for the couple, both of whom are of the Jewish faith. Their wedding followed that summer and featured all of the tradition and ceremony of a Jewish Orthodox union.

TheScene   Design and Décor

Andrea's dream wedding was motivated by her creamy gold satin sash, her love of red roses, and a picture of a tree-lined ceremony aisle. Elements of this Jewish Orthodox wedding included a planned Tish, a Badeken, a Yichud, the ceremony, a cocktail reception, a dinner, after-dinner dancing, a dessert lounge, and midnight munchies.

BrightIdea

Make It Personal

Go the extra mile on every detail by packaging and delivering the personal flowers in style. We had our calligrapher personalize the wedding party's names on tags that adorned their flower boxes.

AfterDinner

....

Gourmet Coffee and Tea Bar

Late-Nite Crêpes Station
with chocolate and fruit

Baklava, Rugalach
and assorted kosher sweets

Peach, Watermelon, Lemon
and mixed berry sorbets

Mini Burgers *with Crispy Potatoes*

Almond Sponge

Above: *Kosher almond favors.* Right: *A convention
center transformed into an elegant ballroom for
five hundred guests.* Facing, Left: *Even the garnish
on the wedding cake plate matched the décor colors.*
Right: *The passed cocktail had wooden stirrers with
the bride and groom's name.*

Almond Sponge *Kosher Wedding Cake*

4 cups cake flour
2 tsps baking powder
1½ tsps baking soda
1½ tsps salt
1½ cups ground almonds
1 lb margarine
3 cups sugar
3 tsps vanilla
8 eggs

Sift dry ingredients together and set aside. Whip together margarine, sugar, and vanilla until light and fluffy. Separate eggs and add egg yolks one at a time till incorporated into the margarine mixture. Add dry ingredients until incorporated. Whip the egg whites until fluffy but not dry. Fold whites into the mixture until incorporated. Lightly grease pans and bake at 325 degrees F for 35 to 40 minutes. *Serves 40 to 50*

Keep it green by using flowers from the ceremony again at the end of the evening. We took apart rose balls during dinner and *boxed them to go* and throw.

According to religious customs, the dance floor was divided to allow one for women and another for men.

Soirée Signatures

Big Weddings

When planning a wedding reception with a large number of guests in attendance, designing clever details can be burdensome.

Form versus function is a continual battle, but here we prevail.

Orchids

Orchids are a floral treasure. They are beautiful, durable, edible, and come in a variety of colors. We love to dress up a simple glass of champagne with one orchid bloom. It just makes it lovely and this detail can be easily accomplished even in large quantities.

Within the Ribbon

Pew markers are nice, but individual name cards work well when it is necessary to seat numerous families and friends correctly. Our calligrapher made cards that we attached to each chair.

Hanging Escort Cards

We suspended the escort cards from ribbons in alphabetical order down a corridor of windows. This made them visually pleasing and accessible for guests to find their name.

Table Number and Guest Book

Our pet peeve at receptions is long lines. Weddings with vast crowds encourage us to invent new concepts within old traditions. We created sign-in guest booklets for each table and used these as the table numbers. It was very efficient! Guests found their tables quickly and had ample time to write wishes for the bride and groom.

HappilyEverAfter

For us, this wedding was both fascinating and fabulous. We became well informed about the traditions and beliefs of the Orthodox Jewish faith and befriended the kindest family. The rabbi even commented that I was the best non-Jewish coordinator in town! Andrea and Nick are a bright and dedicated couple. We foresee the future holding great things for them.

Facing: Bride and groom departing via rickshaw with a red paper parasol. The rickshaw was adorned with a "Mazel Tov" sign. Above: Mother and father of the bride, about to walk their daughter down the aisle. Right: An extra large cake decorated to match Andrea's dress, with coordinating lace and satin ribbon!

Above, Left: *Signage details.* Right: *Handmade bird nest cake topper by Jim Smeal.* Facing, Left: *Escort/butler cards dangle from sticks placed in umbrellas.* Right: *Carter and Fred, exuberant after the ceremony.*

LoveBirds

Carter Samis and Fred Fellers

Mr.andMrs.

A chance meeting over drinks with a mutual friend led Carter and Fred to a long-term romance. Fred proposed three years later with a stunning ring and dinner at the pair's favorite restaurant, Peninsula Grill. On their last "unmarried" date, Fred wowed Carter once again with a gold band designed as a branch—a central theme of Carter and Soirée's décor—and a love letter with a second "Will You Marry Me?"

Facing: *Cocktails on the front lawn of Drayton Hall Plantation.* Left: *The new Mr. and Mrs. Fellers.* Right: *Letterpress ceremony programs.*

TheScene   Design and Décor

Carter knew exactly what she wanted her wedding day reception to look like—an infusion of Tony Duquette meets modern-day wedding. She purchased ikat fabric from Pakistan, which we then transformed into table runners, throw pillows, bar décor, and a band partition. We embellished the Tony Duquette style of natural elements and hues of oranges and grays into hand-pressed printed materials and personalized details.

Bright Idea

Recipe Coasters

We love to incorporate a family or favorite recipe, and there are many different ways to share the recipe with your guests. It can be printed on letterpress coasters, in a welcome-bag booklet, or on a napkin. Dispensing inherited traditions helps personalize your special day.

C&F
11.01.08

Mama Burts'
RUSSIAN TEA RECIPE
It is the best! You will need two large pots...

1ST POT
8 cups of water
3 tsp whole cloves
2 sticks of cinnamon
1 hull of lemon

2ND POT
8 cups water
2 small (6oz.) cans
of pineapple juice
1 medium can frozen
orange juice diluted

OntheMenu

·············

Samis Salad
*mixed greens with shaved parmesan, pomegranate seeds,
and housemade vinaigrette*

Sweet Potato Biscuits

Brined, Smoked Quail
*stuffed with grilled harvest apples, calvados sauce, and fresh chives,
served with anson mills creamy grits, sautéed haricots verts*

Wedding Cake
Carrot Cake

Dessert Table
*pecan and pumpkin pies,
ginger, orange, and red berry macaroons,
chocolate speckled quail eggs, meringue mushrooms,
and a faux bois coconut cake*

Above: *Miniature pecan and pumpkin pies on wood
stumps made a beautiful dessert table.* Right: *Bride and
groom, along with the wedding party, sit under a
wrought-iron conservatory for dinner.* Facing, Left: *Ikat
table runners, Irish linen tablecloths, and matching table
numbers made for a hip table design.* Right: *Passed hors
d'oeuvres with matching signage.*

Sweet Potato Biscuits

These little biscuits were delicious!

3 cups flour
1½ cups light brown sugar
2½ tsps baking powder
½ tsp allspice
1 tsp cinnamon
¾ tsp salt
¼ tsp plus a pinch baking soda
10½ tbs shortening
½ cup buttermilk
1½ cups chilled sweet potato purée

Mix all dry ingredients; add shortening, buttermilk, and sweet potato purée. Mix, but don't overwork, the dough on a floured board. Cut dough into 2-inch rounds or squares with a cutter. Bake at 350 degrees F for 24 minutes—rotate after first 12 minutes. Coat with melted butter when done. *Makes 18 to 20*

To achieve an eco-friendly wedding, *incorporate natural resources and materials*, such as fallen trees, into table centerpieces.

Facing: *My favorite flower piece of the year.*
Right: *Welcome-bag booklets tucked into an envelope.*

SoiréeSignatures

Boutonnieres

Every little detail matters on your big day. We love to deliver even the smallest things in vogue. Hand-tied boutonnieres with tags were distributed to the groomsmen on mood moss.

Drink Stirrers

One natural element used throughout Carter's wedding was wood. We found charming wooden drink stirrers and had her signature bird motif printed on each.

Bridal Bouquet

Carter's bouquet was exquisite. Hand tied with gray dusty miller leaves, silver Brunia, white dahlias, Coral Charm peonies, Sentyna and Giselle spray roses, and Peach Finesse and Versilia roses. Her special request was to have dupioni silk ribbons sewn into pleats.

Family Favors

The Samis family spent quality time together making their grandmother's famous bread and butter pickles to be given away as favors. The delicious pickles were packaged in mason jars with a matching printed tag.

Altarpiece

Another natural floral alternative is to fill a glass pedestal vase with oranges, kumquats, clementines, and eucalyptus. On either side, we placed a smaller glass vase with mood moss and roses to create a spectacular altarpiece.

HappilyEverAfter

For the mother of the bride, who owns a décor boutique and whose younger daughter was getting married in a mere six months, this wedding had a lot to live up to! We felt a huge sense of accomplishment to receive this note from her after the wedding: "Thank you again for such a beautiful weekend. The time and energy you all put into the wedding was incredible. Everything was awesome including the weather. Thanks so much for all of your efforts and hard work."

*Facing: Lovebirds leaving their reception.
Above: Just married signs should be consistent
with all other printed materials. Right: Having
the wedding cake in a birdcage summarized
the evening décor and converted the everyday
cake table into a centerpiece.*

ShortStory

The Wedding Celebration of Brooke Barrett and Ajesh D'Souza

This harborside reception was designed in colors of sand and water. Details from this evening included late-night Velvet Hammers (a drink famous at the bride's hometown country club) served in juice glasses, a quick kiss during the reception, letterpress invitations with a seashell emblem, flower girl baskets trimmed with shells, a five-tier buttercream wedding cake inspired by Sylvia Weinstock, and guest seats fashioned with ribbons—all manifested into a true love story.

Above, Left: *The table setting in hints of varying blues.* Right: *Escort cards with peacock feathers.*
Facing, Left: *Vases of different colors and sizes were filled with Delphinium Orchids and surrounded by eyelet votives.* Right: *The Earnhardts on the front steps of St. Mary's Catholic Church.*

Mr. and Mrs.
Wesley Earnhardt

sweetheart table

AmoréEterno

Katharine Haklisch and Wes Earnhardt

Mr.andMrs.

Following a storybook meeting on a crowded street corner in New York City, Katharine and Wes's romance spanned several years. On Katharine's return from graduate school in London, they traveled to Kiawah Island where Will's sunrise proposal took place on the beach where his bride had summered during her youth. The couple's ceremony was held at the same church where Katharine's parents had married many years before. Afterwards, they entertained guests at Middleton Place in grand Southern style—spiced with a hint of the bride's Italian heritage.

Facing: *A happy bride.* Left: *Hand-tied bridesmaid bouquet in blue.* Right: *Hand-tied groomsman boutonniere.*

TheScene   Design and Décor

Shades of blue, an Italian heritage, childhood memories, and a picturesque venue enticed our senses to achieve Katharine's fantasy wedding. We altered a nondescript carriage house by adding hanging planters of vibrant hydrangeas and elegant white lanterns that created an enchanted glow.

BrightIdea

Personalized Menu Cards

Personal memorabilia included in the menu cards delighted guests at the table. Private anecdotes, a history of the plantation, and photographs from their formative years initiated conversation and laughter. We also had the guests' names calligraphed on the booklets, to serve as place cards, which were sweetly tucked into the dinner napkins.

Family Style

....

Antipasto Salad

Roasted Beef Tenderloin
Carolina gold rice, and fresh pea and sage rice salad

Herb-Roasted Grouper
with capers and a lemon chardonnay sauce

Farfalle Pasta Primavera
with local farm-raised fresh vegetables

Rustic Bread Basket
filled with focaccia, biscuits, cornbread, and flatbread

Wedding Pies
*ginger, peach, almond • blueberry, lime, coconut,
pecan • apple, cranberry, walnut • raspberry frangipane •
strawberry tart*

Above: *Antipasto Salad.* Right: *Displayed
miniature pies, which were served in lieu of
wedding cake.* Facing: *Embroidered napkins
surprised the bride and groom, one bearing
"Amoré" (love) and the other "Eterno" (forever).
The pie that the bride and groom "cut."*

GingerPeachAlmond *Wedding Pie*

Crust	Filling	Topping
2 cups all-purpose flour	6 very ripe peaches	3 tbs minced crystallized ginger
1 tsp salt	1 cup sugar	1 cup all-purpose flour
3 tbs sugar	½ cup tapioca	½ cup crushed toasted almonds
12 tbs cold unsalted butter	¼ tsp nutmeg	¼ cup unsalted butter
6 tbs ice water		

Crust: Have flour, salt, sugar, and butter cold and rub together with your hands to incorporate but still leaving small pieces of butter in the mixture. Lightly toss with ice water. Wrap in plastic and refrigerate, preferably overnight. Roll out and cut to fit tart shells. Prebake tart shells at 350 degrees F for a few minutes until golden.

Filling: Combine all ingredients and fill prebaked tart shells, then bake at 350 degrees F until mixture just begins to bubble.

Topping: Combine ingredients and rub together with your hands to form a crumbly topping mixture. Cover tarts with crumb topping and bake an additional 10 minutes. *Makes 12 (4-inch) tarts*

Keep it green by minimizing the amount of imported flowers you use. *Choose locally sourced vendors* instead, like we did for the amazing hydrangeas.

Facing: Bartenders getting prepared for the guests to arrive. Above: The bride's hand-tied bouquet with miniature cymbidium white cattleya orchids and phalaenopsis orchids.

SoiréeSignatures

It is important for your guests to feel comfortable throughout your event, and this entails having a clear understanding of entrances, where to sit and leave any personal items, and the evening's timeline. Here, an inviting custom tent entrance performed that duty.

Peacocks

Resident peacocks stroll the grounds at Middleton Place Plantation. When the bride visited Middleton with her family as a child, she had a particular affinity for chasing these birds. So, we included them in our décor by finding a wire peacock frame and attaching escort cards with peacock feathers to the tail.

Bride and Groom Chairs

No matter what, the bride and groom chairs need to have something special. Not only did this couple have their own sweetheart table with surprise embroidered napkins, we also made mum kissing balls that garnished both chairs.

Pew Markers

Pew markers can be personalized too. We love to make the ceremony décor into a personal reflection of the couple. We adorned the front gates with the larger floral monograms, but we also made a baby mum "H" for his side and an "E" for her side of the church.

Framed Photograph

As an alternative for the guest book, brides have been requesting objects that may be observed more prominently than just a book on a shelf. For this event, we photographed the panoramic view of the famous Butterfly lakes at the couple's reception venue. We then enlarged the photo and put it on foam core. Guests were asked to sign their John Hancock signature.

Happily Ever After

Even though we had a strong, hardworking team, laid-back clients, and time on our side, we faced some challenges in pulling off the perfection we demand. The day before this wedding, we had an unforeseen torrential downpour that the tent couldn't handle, which in turn flooded the already-laid carpet. With a few other snafus, we had some last-minute scrambling to do! The thing we love best about our service is that no one knows about behind-the-scenes "disasters" except for us!

Facing: *A shared kiss under a live oak tree.* Above: *The bridal party enjoys a walk on the waterfront.*
RIGHT: A timeless father-daughter dance.

Wedding Resources

Under the Oaks Page 11: Bouquet and boutonniere by Soirée by Tara Guérard, *soireebytaraguerard.com*; cake by Sylvia Weinstock, *sylviaweinstock.com*; floral monograms by Soirée, sign-in cards by The Lettered Olive, *theletteredolive.com*. Page 13: Ceremony site décor, lanterns, bouquet, and boutonniere all by Soirée. Page 15: Hanging lanterns, sofas, pendant lamps, floral arrangement, floral pew marker, cabana tent, and floating floral monogram all by Soirée. Page 17: Cheese display by Epting Events, *eptingevents.com*; calligraphed bar menu by Elizabeth Jones Calligraphy, *elizporcher@gmail.com*; floral arrangements by Soirée; 21 Club mini burgers, from the 21 Club, New York City, Chef Michael Lomonaco, *21club.com*; executed by Epting Events. Page 19: "Love Birds" seed packets by Soirée and The Lettered Olive. Page 21: Clockwise from left: cake conservatory, acrylic table, and boxwoods by Soirée; cake by Sylvia Weinstock; mesh rose petal bags by Soirée, letterpress tags by The Lettered Olive; printed cocktail napkins and letterpress ceremony program by The Lettered Olive; Etched Glass champagne flute available through DC Rentals, *dcrental.com*; flip-flops from Old Navy, *oldnavy.com*; pashminas provided by bride; birdcage by Soirée. Page 23: all reception décor by Soirée.

Glamour Girl Page 25: Location, Drayton Hall Plantation, *draytonhall.org*; floral centerpiece by Soirée by Tara Guérard, *soireebytaraguerard.com*; votive holders available through Barreveld International, *barreveld.com*. Page 27: Dress by Carolina Herrera; ceremony décor by Soirée; letterpress ceremony program by The Lettered Olive, *theletteredolive.com*. Page 29: Bouquet by Soirée; custom gobo and ceiling lighting by PDA, *pdastage.com*; tent décor by Soirée; canvas shoe bags by Twelve NYC, *twelvenyc.com*; letterpress tags by The Lettered Olive. Page 31: Wedding cake and stand by Jim Smeal, *weddingcakesbyjimsmeal.com*; banana split cheesecake shots by JBC Catering, *jbccatering.com*; metal dessert stands through Boss Manufacturing, *bossmanufacturing.com*; acrylic menu cards by The Lettered Olive. Page 33: All fabric, lighting, furniture, and florals by Soirée; silver mint julep cups from Wholesale Flowers and Supplies, *flowersandsupplies.com*. Page 35: Clockwise from left: floral accent by Soirée by Tara Guérard; orchid garlands by Soirée; silly string available at *partyplanitsc.com*; custom stickers and letterpress save the dates by The Lettered Olive; Just Married sign by The Lettered Olive, vintage Rolls Royce available through A Star Limo, *astarlimo.com*; tissue paper flowers by Soirée. Page 37: Bride's shoes by Miu Miu.

Short Story Page 39: Caterer, Fish Catering, *patpropllc.com*; printed cocktail napkins and letterpress invitations by The Lettered Olive, *theletteredolive.com*; floral centerpiece by Soirée by Tara Guérard, *soireebytaraguerard.com*; black ceramic vase available at Jamali Garden, *jamaligarden.com*; wedding cake by Jim Smeal, *weddingcakesbyjimsmeal.com*; shadow box by Soirée.

September Splendor Page 41: Location, Mingo Point at Kiawah Island; furniture and custom pillows by Soirée by Tara Guérard, *soireebytaraguerard.com*; letterpress calligraphed table number by The Lettered Olive, *theletteredolive.com*; and Elizabeth Jones calligraphy, *elizporcher@gmail.com*; green glasses and chairs available at Snyder Event Rentals, *snydereventrentals.com*; linens and centerpiece by Soirée; printed paper by The Lettered Olive; ceramic votives from Tag, *tagltd.com*; bouquet and boutonniere by Soirée. Page 43: Ceremony florals and décor by Soirée by Tara Guérard; square vases from Jamali Garden, *jamaligarden.com*; letterpress ceremony programs from The Lettered Olive. Page 45: Wedding cakes by Jim Smeal, *weddingcakesbyjimsmeal.com*; all fabric draping, lighting, décor, and furniture by Soirée; chivari chairs, dinner china, and glassware by Snyder Event Rentals, *snydereventrentals.com*; butler boxes by Soirée, and patterned paper by The Lettered Olive. Page 47: Passed hors d'oeuvres by the Kiawah Island Golf Resort; letterpress menus and seating cards by The Lettered Olive. Page 49: Marshmallow bags by Soirée and The Lettered Olive. Page 51: Clockwise from left: bouquet and fabric wrap by Soirée by Tara Guérard; custom water bottles and guest amenity boxes by Soirée and The Lettered Olive; custom cookies by Three Smart Cookies, *3smartcookies.net;* "Very Charleston" hardback book available through book retailers; two-sided guest cards by The Lettered Olive; ring bearer pillow by Soirée; flower girl headband and Low Country Lemonade by Soirée; clear glass bottles from Specialty Bottles, *specialty bottles.com;* galvanized bottle holders from Pottery Barn, *potterybarn.com;* lemonade tag by The Lettered Olive and Elizabeth Jones Calligraphy, *elizporcher@gmail.com.* Page 52: Fabric chair backs by Soirée; flags from Flags! Georgia, *unflags.com.*

Wedding Rice Page 71: Floral wreath by Soirée by Tara Guérard, *soireebytaraguerard.com;* monogrammed sign by The Lettered Olive, *theletteredolive.com;* bridesmaids' bouquets by Soirée; wedding cake by Jim Smeal, *weddingcakesbyjimsmeal. com.* Page 73: Bridal portraits by Liz Banfield photography, *lizbanfield.com;* floral wall and pendant lamp by Soirée; clear-top tent by Snyder Event Rentals, *snydereventrentals.com;* bridal flowers by Soirée; horse and carriage by Charleston Coach, *charlestoncoach.com.* Page 75: Banquettes, linens, and pillows by Soirée; acrylic lamps from Kravet, *kravet.com;* chandeliers from Solaria, *solaria-home.com;* benches, fabric, and tent edging by Soirée; coffee tables from Ikea, *ikea.com;* bridal bouquet and monogrammed ribbon by Soirée. Page 77: Catering by JBC Catering, *jbccatering.com;* reception location Boone Hall Plantation, *boonehallplantation;* lace rimmed plates available through Snyder Event Rentals, *snydereventrentals.com;* take-out boxes through Paper Mart, *papermart.com.* Page 79: Pendant lamps, acrylic tables, votives, and flowers by Soirée; wedding cakes by Jim Smeal; custom M&M's at *mymms.com.* Page 81: Clockwise from top left: letterpress invitations by The Lettered Olive; tent draping and ottomans by Soirée; restroom trailers by Nature's Calling, *naturescallinginc.com;* sign-in cards by The Lettered Olive; facing: wedding rice bags and tags by Soirée and The Lettered Olive; floral wall by Soirée. Page 83: Pendant lamps, linens, flowers, and votives by Soirée.

Night Before Page 69: Clockwise from top left: printed butler cards by The Lettered Olive, *theletteredolive.com;* orange bottles from Accent Décor, *accentdecor.com;* printed menu cards and printed invitations by The Lettered Olive; caterer, McCrady's Restaurant, *mccradysrestaurant.com;* facing: paper lanterns from Pearl River Mart, *pearlriver.com;* ribbon and flowers by Soirée.

Bands of Gold Page 71: Invitation with engraved bellyband by The Lettered Olive, *theletteredolive.com;* fabric curtains, furniture, and custom pillows by Soirée by Tara Guérard, *soireebytaraguerard.com;* etched glasses from Vieuxtemps, *vieuxtemps.net.* Page 73: Wedding cake by Jim Smeal, *weddingcakesbyjimsmeal.com;* custom ring bearer pillow by Soirée; bride's dress by Badgley Mischka, through Gown Boutique of Charleston, *gownboutiqueofcharleston.com.* Page 75: Trees, furniture, and all lighting by Soirée; printed favor boxes by The Lettered Olive; flavored French macaroons by A Matter of Taste, *amatteroftastecharleston@hotmail.com.* Page 77: Patterned paper and tag by The Lettered Olive; calligraphy by Elizabeth Jones Calligraphy, *elizporcher@gmail. com;* printed street names by The Lettered Olive; floral balls, trees, and custom linens by Soirée; chairs, glassware, and china from Snyder Event Rentals, *snydereventrentals.com;* drink signs by The Lettered Olive. Page 79: Dance floor and gold chairs from Snyder Event Rentals; all fabric draping, florals, and lighting from Soirée; gold ribbon from Midori Ribbon, *midoriribbon.com.* Page 81: Clockwise from left: pashminas found in Chinatown, New York; bride's bouquet by Soirée (cameo bride's own); custom logo on matchboxes by The Lettered Olive; matchboxes available at For Your Party, *foryourparty.com;* facing: chair décor by Soirée; furniture rentals from Snyder Lounge, *snyderlounge.com;* pendant lamps from Brocade Home, *brocadehome.com.* Page 83: Sparklers from Big Dave's Fireworks, Hollywood, South Carolina.

Sea Island Soirée Page 85: Bride's bouquet by Soirée by Tara Guérard, *soireebytaraguerard.com;* wedding cake by Jim Smeal, *weddingcakesbyjimsmeal.com;* tent through Beachview Tent Rentals, *beachviewtentrentals.com;* location Ocean Forest Golf Club at Sea Island, Georgia. Page 87: Bride's dress by Rivini through Mark Ingram Atelier, *bridalatelier;* floral wreaths and bridesmaids' bouquets by Soirée; bridesmaids' dresses by Jenny Yoo, *jennyyoo.com.* Page 89: Flowers, décor, furniture, and lighting by Soirée; wedding cake by Jim Smeal, *weddingcakesbyjimsmeal.com;* palm hand fans from *favorsandflowers.com;* printed tags by The Lettered Olive, *theletteredolive.com.* Page 91: Printed menus and place cards by The Lettered Olive; woven seagrass chargers through Snyder Event Rentals, *snydereventrentals.com;* sand dollars at US Shell, *usshell.com;* catering through Ocean Forest Golf Club. Page 93: Seagrass tent ceiling, custom pillows, and furniture all by Soirée; square glass vases at Accent Decor, *accentdecor.com;* candles available at Tag, *tagltd.com;* starfish at Jamali Garden, *jamaligarden.com.* Page 95: Clockwise from left: seashell drink stirrers and shadow box bars by Soirée; starfish available at Jamali Garden; sand dollars from US Shell; printed drink signs by The Lettered Olive; facing: shell table names and butler cards by The Lettered Olive. Page 97: Printed sign and cards by The Lettered Olive; shell bowl at Anthropologie, *anthropologie.com;* flowers by Soirée; printed cake boxes by The Lettered Olive.

Night Before Page 98: Clockwise from top left: lanterns by Soirée, *soireebytaraguerard.com;* glass compote bowls and apothecary jars from Abigails, *abigails.net;* butler cards by The Lettered Olive, *theletteredolive.com;* carved pumpkin by Soirée by Tara Guérard; take-out boxes from US Box, *usbox. com;* facing: location, The Confederate Home and College, *scocr.org.*

Warm and Fuzzy Page 101: Printed tag and paper from The Lettered Olive, *theletteredolive.com;* cake by Publix; feathered table number by Soirée by Tara Guérard, *soireebytaraguerard.com;* wooden chairs available through Snyder Event Rentals, *snydereventrentals.com;* bride's bouquet by Soirée. Page 103: Flowers by Soirée. Page 105: Monogrammed chair cover and cabana tent by Soirée; white votives from Tag, *tagltd.com;* monogrammed ribbon by Soirée. Page 107: Printed candy bar wrappers, tags, and vase wrap by The Lettered Olive; woven chargers available through Snyder Event Rentals; custom meatball picks by The Lettered Olive; catering by Erimic Associates Catering. Page 109: Boutonnieres and tray by Soirée; hot chocolate display by Soirée; chocolate swizzle sticks from Harris Teeter; floral arrangement by Soirée. Page 111: Candy bar wrappers by The Lettered Olive; ring bearer pillow by Soirée; flower girl headpiece and printed box by Soirée; children's boxes by Soirée/The Lettered Olive. Page 113: Furniture rentals through Snyder Lounge, *snyderlounge.com.*

Eyelet Evening Page 115: Bride's dress by Carolina Herrera; glass cylinders available through Accent Décor, *accentdécor.com;* bridesmaid bouquet by Soirée by Tara Guérard, *soireebytaraguerard.com;* wedding cake by Jim Smeal, *weddingcakesbyjimsmeal.com.* Page 117: Bride's bouquet and flower girl headband by Soirée; location: Drayton Hall Plantation, *draytonhall.org.* Page 119: Place card and menu by The Lettered Olive, *theletteredolive.com;* eyelet china charger through Snyder Event Rentals, *snydereventrentals. com;* pendant lamps through CB2, *cb2.com;* calligraphed table number by Elizabeth Jones Calligraphy, *elizporcher@gmail.com;* ceiling draping, eyelet lamps, custom linens, furniture, and centerpieces all by Soirée; pillows at West Elm, *westelm.com;* square glass votives at Jamali Garden, *jamaligarden.com;* eyelet drink umbrellas by Soirée. Page 121: Floral centerpieces by Soirée; white vases through Jamali Garden, *jamaligarden. com;* chairs, glassware, silverware, and white china through Snyder Event Rentals; catering by JBC Catering, *jbccatering. com;* sign by Soirée and The Lettered Olive. Page 123: Bouquet, flower girl headpieces, and flower girl pouches all by Soirée; market umbrellas available through Snyder Lounge, *snyderlounge.com;* ottomans and hanging candles by Soirée. Page 125: Clockwise from left: printed favor cards by The Lettered Olive; ceremony décor by Soirée; letterpress invitations by The Lettered Olive; facing: "wishes that stick" box by Soirée; magnetic place cards by The Lettered Olive;

magnets at Custom Engraving, *customengraving.com*. Page 127: Bride's bouquet by Soirée.

ShortStory Page 129: Clockwise from top left: mr. and mrs. cookies through 3 Smart Cookies, *3smartcookies.net*; bride's bouquet by Soirée, *soireebytaraguerard.com*; cake by Jim Smeal, *weddingcakesbyjimsmeal.com*; mr. and mrs. printed napkins by The Lettered Olive, *theletteredolive.com*; church location First Scots Presbyterian Church; printed cards by The Lettered Olive, *theletteredolive.com*; facing: bridal bouquet by Soirée.

RosesareRed Page 131: Ceiling draping and red lanterns by Soirée by Tara Guérard, *soireebytaraguerard.com*; hanging rose balls by Soirée; bride's dress by Monique Lhuillier; letterpress invitations by The Lettered Olive, *theletteredolive.com*. Page 133: Custom chuppa and hanging lanterns by Soirée; rose bouquet by Soirée. Page 135: Etched glasses available through DC Rental, *dcrental.com*; birch trees and décor by Soirée; calligraphed flower tags by Elizabeth Jones Calligraphy, *elizporcher@gmail.com*. Page 137: Jordan almond favors and tags by Soirée and The Lettered Olive; draping, lanterns, and cabana tents by Soirée; kosher cake by Jim Smeal, *weddingcakesbyjimsmeal.com*; drink tags by The Lettered Olive. Page 139: Leather furniture and dance floor through Snyder Event Rentals, *snydereventrentals.com*; décor and flowers by Soirée; rose petals to go by Soirée and The Lettered Olive; gold take-out containers available through Paper Mart, *papermart.com*. Page 141: Clockwise from left: etched glass available through DC Rentals, *dcrentals.com*; hanging butler cards from The Lettered Olive; calligraphed place cards from Elizabeth Jones Calligraphy; sign-in book by Soirée. Page 143: Rickshaw available through Charleston Rickshaw Company, *charlestonrickshaw.com*; kosher wedding cake by Jim Smeal.

LoveBirds Page 145: Speckled eggs available through Knipschildt Chocolatier, *knipschildt.net*; bird signage through The Lettered Olive, *theletteredolive.com*; cake topper by Jim Smeal, *weddingcakesbyjimsmeal.com*. Page 147: Location Drayton Hall Plantation, *draytonhall.org*; furniture by Soirée by Tara Guérard, *soireebytaraguerard.com*; umbrellas available through Snyder Lounge, *snyderlounge.com*; bride's dress by Carolina Herrera; letterpress ceremony program by The Lettered Olive. Page 149: Place card and menus by The

Lettered Olive; orange and white ribbon available through The Ribbon Factory Outlet, *ribbonoutlet.com*; venetian plates available through Snyder Event Rentals, *snydereventrentals.com*; floral arrangement and reception décor by Soirée; antlers provided by bride; white lamp available at IKEA, *ikea.com*; ikat pillows and fabric on Ebay; Moroccan tea cups through Barreveld International, *barreveld.com*; letterpress coasters by The Lettered Olive. Page 151: Miniature pies by Jim Smeal; wrought-iron conservatory through Soirée; printed table number by The Lettered Olive and Elizabeth Jones Calligraphy, *elizporcher@gmail.com*; ikat fabric available on Ebay; catering by Good Food Catering, *goodfoodcatering.net*; food sign by The Lettered Olive. Page 153: Floral arrangement by Soirée; hand-blown glass candlesticks from Abigail's, *abigails.net*; taper candles from Creative Candles, *creativecandles.com*; guest booklets and tags by The Lettered Olive; gravel-colored paper sleeves through Paper Source, *paper-source.com*; stirrers available at For Your Party, *foryourparty.com*; drink sign from The Lettered Olive; facing: letterpress tags from The Lettered Olive; bread and butter pickles supplied by mother of the bride; glass vases available at Abigail's; altar décor by Soirée. Page 161: Clockwise from top left: boutonnieres by Soirée by Tara Guérard; bride's bouquet and pleated ribbon by Soirée; drink stirrers and signage by The Lettered Olive; wooden stirrers available through For Your Party; facing: letterpress tags from The Lettered Olive; bread and butter pickles and jars supplied by the mother of the bride; large glass vases through Abigail's; altar décor and flowers by Soirée. Page 157: Just Married sign by Soirée; wedding cake by Jim Smeal.

ShortStory Page 159: Letterpress invites by The Lettered Olive, *theletteredolive.com*; ribbon from Midori, *midoriribbon.com*; leather furniture available at Snyder Lounge, *snyderlounge.com*; cake by Jim Smeal, *weddingcakesbyjimsmeal.com*; flower girl basket by Soirée by Tara Guérard, *soireebytaraguerard.com*; hanging lamps from CB2, *cb2.com*; fabric draping and flowers by Soirée.

AmoréEterno Page 161: Blue glasses and china available through Snyder Event Rentals, *snydereventrentals.com*; printed menus through The Lettered Olive, *theletteredolive.com*; fabric runners through Soirée by Tara Guérard, *soireebytaraguerard.com*; calligraphed butler cards

by The Lettered Olive and Elizabeth Jones Calligraphy, *elizporcher@gmail.com*; peacock feathers at Plumes N' Feathers, *plumesnfeathers.com*; flowers by Soirée; glass bottles from Pottery Barn, *potterybarn.com*; votive holders from Design Ideas, *designideas.net*; floral monograms by Soirée; church location St. Mary's Catholic Church, *catholic-doc.org*. Page 163: Bride's bouquet and boutonnieres from Soirée by Tara Guérard; bride's dress by Alvina Valenta; groomsmen ties from Vineyard Vines, *vineyardvines.com*. Page 165: Lanterns from West Elm, *westelm.com*; floral arrangements by Soirée; blue and clear glass bottles from Pottery Barn, *potterybarn.com*; furniture and custom pillows by Soirée; printed menu booklet by The Lettered Olive. Page 167: Catering by Events by Stephen Duvall, *eventsbyduvall.com*; pie tags by The Lettered Olive and Soirée; mini pies by Jim Smeal, *weddingcakesbyjimsmeal.com*; white metal dessert stand through Boss Manufacturing, *bossmanufacturing.com*; monogrammed napkins by Soirée; eyelet china plates available through Snyder Event Rentals; pie by Jim Smeal; pie signage by Elizabeth Jones Calligraphy. Page 169: All furniture and pillows through Soirée; bride's bouquet and floral arrangements from Soirée. Page 171: Clockwise from top left: tent by Boutique Tents by REDUX; floral balls from Soirée; ribbon from Midori, *midoriribbon.com*; wire peacock from Pottery Barn; peacock feathers through Plumes N' Feathers; facing: floral monogram from Soirée; calligraphed tag from Elizabeth Jones Calligraphy.

Soirée Inc. by Tara Guérard coordinates, plans, and designs weddings and events with offices based out of Charleston and New York City. Available for travel. We can be contacted at 843.577.5006 in Charleston and 646.329.6258 in New York, or www.soireebytaraguerard.com. Our sister company, The Lettered Olive, creates custom stationery suites for all occasions. For more information call 800.558.0667 or visit www.theletteredolive.com.